CLASSIC MARQUES

Citroën Cars
1945-1964

MALCOLM BOBBITT

NOSTALGIA ROAD

First published by Crécy Publishing Ltd 2011

A CIP record for this book is available from the British Library

ISBN 9 781908 34700 8

Printed in Malta by Melita Press

Crécy Publishing Limited
1a Ringway Trading Estate
Shadowmoss Road
Manchester M22 5LH

www.crecy.co.uk

Front Cover: The DS model seen here illustrates Citroën's radical styling and innovative technology. The vehicle illustrated was built in Britain at Citroën's Slough factory in 1961 and used on official company business including press and publicity work. *Malcolm Bobbitt*

Rear Cover Top: A 1954 six-cylinder British (Slough) built Traction Avant. *Bottom:* An early 2CV bearing the scars of a long and hard life. *Malcolm Bobbitt*

Contents Page: The iconic DS is as much a part of French style and culture as the Eiffel Tower. When it was introduced in 1955, this Citroën was the most advanced car in the world. *Citroën*

Acknowledgements

THE author is grateful to the following who have contributed to this book, including permission to use photographic material: Citroën UK, Citroën Car Club, Andrew Minney, David Conway, Nigel Somerset-Leeke, Guy Pursey, Richard Mann, Brian Scott-Quinn, Tony Stokoe, Brian Chandler, Bill Wolf, Shotaro Kobayashi and the BBC.

CONTENTS

Introduction

FEW car manufacturers have made such an impact on society as that demonstrated by Citroën. Bearing the famous Double Chevron insignia that has been synonymous with the marque since 1919, Citroën's Traction Avant significantly influenced automobile technology when it was introduced in 1934. Not only did the revolutionary design feature front-wheel drive, it incorporated all-round hydraulic braking, torsion bar suspension and chassis-less construction.

Renowned for innovative engineering, Citroën also addressed the need for an inexpensive means of transportation during post-war austerity. With its unbelievable level of frugality, their 2CV sold in huge numbers despite its fragile looks. With minimal power derived from a two-cylinder air-cooled engine, the capacity of which would not have been out of place on a lawn mower, the 2CV had the ability to cope with the roughest terrain, courtesy of the most enduring suspension.

Citroën innovation really came under the spotlight in 1955 when the extraordinary DS was launched. Adventurous use of technology meant that hydraulics assisted gear selection, steering and braking as well as providing a means of suspension that nearly six decades later is still superior to anything else.

In addition to building cars, Citroën also made a wide range of commercial vehicles, including the H-van, which was as Gallic as baguettes and Gauloise cigarettes. Less appreciated is Citroën's significant contribution to Britain's motor industry, when it assembled cars at Slough over a period of 40-years.

Malcolm Bobbitt
Cockermouth, 2011

Two generations of Citroën are seen here, the vehicle in the background being a 1955 example of the Traction Avant that entered production in 1934. Near the camera is an early example of the DS, which was introduced to huge acclaim in the autumn of 1955. Both vehicles were assembled in Britain. *Malcolm Bobbitt*

Despite its utilitarian appearance, the 2CV won many friends who appreciated its economy, comfort and reliability. In the background can be seen an Ami 6, an up-market version of the Deux Chevaux. Sharing its sibling's simple technology, the controversially-styled Ami was often labelled the ugliest car in the world but nevertheless proved to be highly popular. *Malcolm Bobbitt*

Left-hand page: With its characteristic styling and corrugated body panels, the front-wheel drive H-van was a familiar sight throughout Europe. It was the choice of farmers, market traders and business users wanting a commodious vehicle. *Malcolm Bobbitt*

Front-Wheel Drive

Wﮨﮯﮟ Citroën resumed car production in the shadow of World War II, there was only one model in the catalogue, the Traction Avant. Considerably more modern in concept than most other vehicles then available, Citroën's front-wheel drive models had first been put into production in 1934, when they were hailed as being a breakthrough in design and technology. On introduction, the Traction Avant had also displayed a number of features that, whilst modern, were not entirely novel; chassis-less construction, front-wheel drive, torsion bar suspension and hydraulic braking had all been tried with varying degrees of success. What made the rakishly-styled Citroën so remarkable was that it was the first mass-produced car to employ all of these features.

It would be accurate to say that the Citroën models announced prior to the Traction Avant were built using mass production techniques but were otherwise largely conventional in their construction.

The first cars to carry the now familiar Double Chevron insignia had been introduced in 1919 and featured normal chassis arrangements. André Citroën's penchant for innovative engineering had brought mass-production car-making to Europe; he was the first motor manufacturer on the continent to use all-steel bodies and incorporated Chrysler's 'floating power' vibration insulated engine mountings to good effect, thus building cars that were eminently satisfying to drive.

An entrepreneur in the fullest sense, Citroën was a genius when it came to publicity. Illuminating the Eiffel Tower for a decade between 1924 and 1934, Citroën's name (in 100-foot high letters) was visible from a distance of 30 miles. Other publicity feats that Le Patron inaugurated were taxi and coach services throughout France in order that his name became a by-word for efficient public transport systems, whilst he also sponsored a number of outstanding geographical missions to explore the Sahara Desert, darkest Africa, the Himalayas and China. The expeditions were conducted by some of the most experienced scientists of the time and were undertaken using specially designed half-tracked Citroën-Kegresse vehicles capable of negotiating all types of terrain.

With his Traction Avant, Citroën was to influence automotive technology for generations to come. It was a car that was strikingly modern in appearance, employing a shape sculptured by the Italian Flamino Bertoni. Characteristics were a low centre of gravity, the absence of running boards and, all the more pertinent, a performance that was as sure-footed as its streamlined shape. It wasn't all good news, however: developing the car had been a desperately costly business!

It was also beset with technical problems, so much so that it drained Citroën's finances and then led to the firm's collapse in 1935. Owing to the urgency in launching the new car, thereby aiming to gain a significant lead over his rivals and replenishing company finances, the Traction Avant was prematurely introduced, the consequence being that many technical problems had still to be addressed. A major factor in the rush to launch the car had been Le Patron's health; the diagnosis of incurable stomach cancer had worsened a frantic situation.

Not withstanding the fact that the Traction Avant was hurriedly put into production, it was, in essence, a ground-breaking design offering those who drove it an altogether new motoring experience. The car's interior was also radical, the monocoque construction allowing occupants to be spaciously accommodated, whilst the suspension afforded the most comfortable ride.

Introduced in 1934, the Traction Avant was seen as being the most advanced car then produced. Sold in France as the Citroën 7, it was marketed in Britain as the Twelve. This period publicity photograph is the same as that used in France, close scrutiny of the picture reveals that the original image has been reversed in order to depict right hand drive. *Citroën publicity*

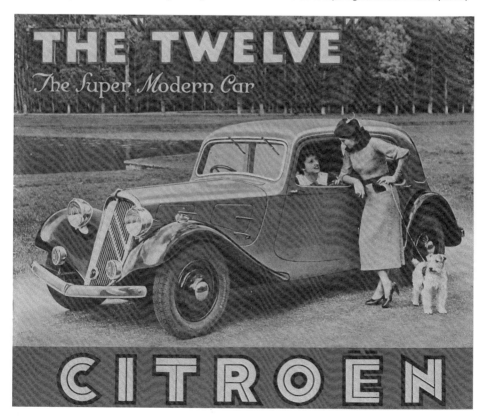

The busy end of the Traction Avant, showing the position of the engine and gearbox, the latter forwardly placed and vulnerable in the event of a frontal impact. Evident too are the drive shafts, and these are important to illustrate as Citroën was pioneering a mass-produced front-wheel drive car. *Citroën*

Below Right: The scene at Quai de Javel, Citroën's vast factory located alongside the River Seine in Paris where production of the Traction Avant is clearly seen under way. The date is the mid-1930s; note the modern technology employed at the works. *Citroën*

Below: Pictured in Paris in the early 1930s with a Citroën 7, François Lecot (left) and Maurice Penaud are about to embark on a marathon non-stop tour of France and Belgium. Lecot is famed for his 400,000km reliability trial in a similar car. *Citroën*

Owing to front-wheel drive, the three-speed gearbox was vulnerably positioned ahead of the engine, gear changing courtesy of an oddly-shaped selector (universally known as the 'mustard spoon'); this sprouted from the dashboard to operate a system of long levers. Despite the seemingly convoluted selector mechanism, it was, nevertheless, an efficient arrangement, albeit gear changing was not to be hurried. The gearbox fitted to the car had been quickly contrived and was not the type originally proposed. It was André Citroën's wish that an automatic gearbox be specified, but this took too long to perfect, hence the arguably conventional type was ultimately fitted.

An early Traction Avant pictured in Paris with an obvious over-heating problem. Though the Traction proved to be a reliable vehicle, its introduction was beset with difficulties, mainly due to it being prematurely launched. Development of the Traction aggravated Citroën's financial collapse and its subsequent acquisition by Michelin, whose investment made it possible to perfect the design. *Author's collection*

The Traction's low centre of gravity, coupled with front-wheel drive, meant that its handling and road-holding characteristics were unlike any other car. It could be driven through bends and corners at previously impossible speeds, and Citroën's sales personnel lost no time in demonstrating to potential customers that this was 'the car that could not be overturned'. Publicity material put the Citroën two-years ahead of its rivals, but in truth it was actually far more advanced, especially considering that Alec Issigonis's Mini (produced by BMC) was not launched until 26th August 1959.

Following Citroën's collapse, the car-maker was acquired by Michelin, its principal creditor. Recognising the Traction Avant's importance, Citroën's new owner immediately injected the necessary investment to perfect its design. Pierre Michelin and Pierre Boulanger were installed at Javel, Citroën's Paris factory, to manage the car-making enterprise, Boulanger being appointed chairman on Michelin's premature death in 1937. Problems with the Traction were not insurmountable, and, if only André Citroën had agreed to give the project more development time, no doubt the teething troubles could have been addressed prior to the vehicle's launch.

Due to the car's stability and performance, along with the benefits of front-wheel drive, monocoque bodyshell and low centre of gravity, the Traction Avant was used by both gangsters and police. During the war years the car acquired a synonymy with the French Resistance and later became a symbol of liberation, as depicted in this emotive picture. *Citroën*

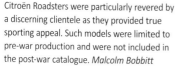

Citroën Roadsters were particularly revered by a discerning clientele as they provided true sporting appeal. Such models were limited to pre-war production and were not included in the post-war catalogue. *Malcolm Bobbitt*

Work on the car quickly progressed under the direction of André Lefèbvre, the brilliant young engineer enlisted by Citroën to oversee work on the radical design. Lefèbvre was well acquainted with innovative methods of engineering, having worked with maverick French motor and aircraft designer Gabriel Voisin. Both Lefèbrve and Bertoni were to enjoy significant careers with Citroën and between them they were responsible for the emergence of two other iconic cars, the 2CV and DS.

Feverish work conducted over a few months was sufficient to overcome the Traction's problems. The body shells, which had a tendency to split apart, were suitably strengthened, drive shafts with a propensity to snap like matchsticks were re-engineered, and engines that were under powered and prone to overheating were re-designed. New and larger-engined models were announced and compared to the original cars with their 1,303cc engines, the 1,529cc, 1,628cc and 1,911cc two-litre models afforded considerably enhanced performance. Sadly Le Patron's untimely death in July 1935 at the age of 56 meant that he was denied seeing the fruits of his endeavours.

Traction Avant cars were fitted with a variety of engines, the most widely specified being the 1,911cc unit introduced in the autumn of 1934. Cars were not only built in France but also in Belgium and at Slough in the United Kingdom. Slough cars were not only used in this country but also exported to British Empire (later Commonwealth) countries including South Africa, from where this image originates. *Citroën publicity*

The decision was taken to broaden the type of body styles available so that in addition to the initial Légère (light) saloon there appeared a long wheelbase version with a wider track, examples of which were known as Normales. A Roadster also became available, along with a Coupé and Faux-cabriolet.

Other body configurations on a stretched platform included a Limousine, a seven- to eight-seater Familiale with two or three (according to specification) folding forward-facing occasional seats and a Commerciale, the latter featuring a split tailgate. Most adventurous was a prototype 3.8-litre V8 Super-Traction (the '22'), which, though built in prototype form, failed to go into production. Recognising the need for a grand tourer, a 2,867cc six-cylinder model was offered for 1939, in Saloon, Limousine and Familiale body styles (a single Cabriolet was also built) with production continuing until 1940.

The ancestry of Citroën's front-wheel drive monocoque design can be traced to 1931 when Le Patron visited America. His itinerary included a meeting with the Budd organisation of Philadelphia, from whom Citroën had negotiated the rights to build his all-steel motor bodies in 1924.

There he was shown a revolutionary design that obviously excited his philosophy towards innovative engineering. Moreover, Citroën recognised that such a product would place him appreciably ahead of his rivals in terms of vehicle design and technology, and thus boost sales. Preparing for the Traction Avant at Javel had, however, been a painfully slow business, owing to the huge technological forward leap involved.

The problems in production continued, and it was only on the arrival of Lefèbvre and Bertoni that the design process was able to progress rapidly. However, in contrast, the post-war Traction Avant prospered from a number of technical modifications introduced since the production had commenced in 1934. Improvements were made to the transmission in respect of gearbox and drive

It was not only Europe that clamoured for the front-wheel drive Citroën; in Japan the Traction Avant was highly regarded. Here that country's foremost motoring writer, Shotaro Kobayashi, is pictured with his car amidst a wintry scene. *Shotaro Kobayashi*

It was radical in styling and design in the 1930s but by the mid-1950s the Traction Avant was arguably showing its age. Technically, however, it remained considerably more advanced than most of its contemporaries. The centre car shown here is a Slough-built Light 15, the others being longer wheelbase French Normale and (right) a French Légère.

shafts, torsion bar suspension and, in 1936, adoption of rack and pinion steering. Styling arrangements changed little, the most obvious being an externally-opening boot from October 1935, the adoption of slightly wider wings and, from May 1946, removal of opening ports in favour of louvres along the bonnet sides for cooling purposes, a feature of the pre-war six-cylinder cars.

During World War II Javel suffered badly from German and Allied bombings in 1940, 1943 and 1944. With the war over, France, like Britain, lacked resources and raw materials, but amazingly car production at Javel resumed in June 1945, albeit somewhat slowly and with a single model, the 1,911cc 11CV Onze Légère. For those customers who were disappointed that the catalogue no longer supported Cabriolet or Coupé models, there was the thorny proposition of finding suitable pre-war examples. The Traction Avant models built during the first year of post-war production suffered from materials starvation, many cars leaving the factory unfinished and minus their spare wheels, some even devoid of tyres. Two colour schemes were offered, light or dark metallic grey, while matching cloth seats and pressed cardboard door panels added to the austerity.

There was no lack of customers who had already discovered the Traction's virtues, however, even to the point that during the war the car had become synonymous with

The scene could have been Paris but it is actually Glamis Castle in Perthshire. The evocative styling of the Traction models, with chevrons emblazoned across their radiators, is seen to good effect; these cars once a familiar sight on French roads. Nearest the camera is the revolutionary DS that was introduced in 1955, this being a post-1967 model with its revised frontal styling. *Malcolm Bobbitt*

gangsters, the police and, not least, the French Resistance. In fashion with Britain's early post-war motor industry, French production was largely exported to earn foreign currency, and less than 25% of Traction Avant output was made available to the home market. It was not until February 1946 that production of the longer wheelbase 15CV six-cylinder-engined car (known as La Reine de la Route) resumed in limited numbers, 203 examples leaving the factory by the year-end.

Thirteen months later, the Onze Normale entered production, 1,698 cars having been built by the end of 1947. Specification changes remained minimal until the summer of 1952, by which time Michelin's Pilote wheels (which were also fitted to some other French cars) had given way to less expensive disc wheels. There were a number of minor design modifications, including a revised bumper arrangement incorporating over riders; headlamps had painted rather than chromed shells.

By the late 1940s black had become the optimum vehicle colour. Interior trim arrangements underwent change: front seats with their chrome tubular rails were replaced by those more lavishly upholstered, and facias were updated to give an art deco flavour.

Later mainly black paintwork gave way to greater colour choice. Another criticism of the Traction Avant had been its limited boot space, the flush-fitting drop-down cover accommodating the spare wheel, and this was addressed in July 1952 when Citroën devised a lift-up boot lid, swollen in shape supposedly to provide greater luggage capacity.

Rather than the spare wheel being carried externally, it was internally located in an upright position, proving to be an encumbrance when stowing and accessing luggage. The new boot arrangement was adopted over the entire range of cars which, for the 1954 model year, was widened to include a new version of the Familiale, in both four- and six-cylinder derivations. A Commerciale derivative was additionally re-introduced, exclusively on the four-cylinder cars, the split tailgate giving way to a top-hinged one-piece affair. The extra-length wheelbase cars found willing customers, especially as the Familiale anticipated the emergence of the modern multi-purpose vehicle. The Commerciale's specification comprised removable rear seats and a height adjustable floor to offer business users and farmers unequalled carrying capacity, and can be claimed as being the precursor to the modern estate car.

The shape of the Traction Avant changed relatively little during production. The earliest cars were without external boot access, the drop-down cover being introduced in 1935. The styling depicted here remained until 1952, when a larger boot arrangement was devised. *Brian Scott-Qiunn*

Running boards never featured on the Traction Avant owing to the car's integral construction (though kits could be obtained), as the vehicle's low profile allowed for easy entry into and out of the cabin. *Malcolm Bobbitt*

In the post-war years both the Légère (light) and Normale models were powered by the tough if not slightly agricultural 1,911cc engine and were noted for their keen performance. Both models (shown here is a Normale) were given a modified boot arrangement in 1952, the lift-up trunk revealing the spare wheel, which had to be removed when loading bulky items. *Malcolm Bobbitt*

Two other important changes to the model line-up became apparent. Firstly, in May 1954, to coincide with the Traction's 20th anniversary, a new six-cylinder car, the 15-6H, made its debut. Then, a year later, a new four-cylinder engine, the 11D, was introduced to give the Légère and Normale a small but welcome increase in power. The additions to the model range were significant in their own right.

The 15-6H (H denoting Hydraulique) featured a new suspension arrangement on the rear axle, the torsion bars being replaced by self-levelling hydropneumatics, a design perfected by Citroën engineers over a number of years. The mode of suspension caught the attention of the motoring press, and for good reason as it transformed the Traction Avant's already superlative ride into something even more outstanding. The Hydraulique model quickly won acclaim when, as part of a publicity stunt, a member of Citroën's marketing team opened a bottle of champagne and served it without spilling a drop whilst the car was travelling at speed.

Operated by a drive taken from the engine, the suspension worked on a system of fluid pumped under pressure from a main under-bonnet accumulator to gas-filled spheres at the rear wheels. The fitting of height correctors meant that during normal driving conditions, and that includes being stationary with the engine idling, a constant height was maintained, irrespective of the vehicle's load. The car's ride was such that it had an ability to float over the roughest surfaces.

In order for the 15-6H to afford the best ride and handling characteristics, it was necessary to soften the front suspension by lengthening the torsion bars forwards, and adding an anti-roll bar. Not evident though was the fact that the 15-6H was a test-bed for the forthcoming DS to be announced in Paris in October 1955. Production of the 15-6H ceased on announcement of the DS. The 11D engine was another modification intended for the yet to be announced DS. Having the same cubic capacity as previously, but with rotation to the right (droit) instead of to the left, the output rose from 56 to 65bhp owing to several design modifications including provision of a new cylinder head, modified camshaft, big-end bearings and attention to valve gear.

The Traction was built with a variety of wheelbase lengths and body configurations. Depicted here is the long wheelbase Commerciale, which post-war had a full-length opening tailgate giving access to a spacious interior. *Malcolm Bobbitt*

The Commerciale had rear seats, which when folded helped form a flat floor in the style of the modern hatchback or estate car. *Malcolm Bobbitt*

Post-war Traction cars had cooling louvres along the bonnet flanks as depicted on this late example. Pre-war cars were fitted with opening ports, though six-cylinder models always carried this arrangement. Except for the earliest examples, post-war cars had windscreen wipers fixed to the scuttle rather than above the screen. *Malcolm Bobbitt*

The six-cylinder Traction cars were always revered for their performance and comfort, and none more so than the 15-Six H with its hydropneumatic self-levelling rear suspension. Introduced in June 1938, post-war production commenced in February 1946, the 15H with its exceptional ride quality being built from April 1954 as a test-bed for the forthcoming DS. Pictured here is a Slough-built car. *Malcolm Bobbitt*

The performance wasn't exactly ground-breaking, but the higher compression of 6.8:1 compared to 6.5:1 did at least help to improve acceleration, provide a maximum of 50mph in second gear and squeeze a further 2mph top speed to afford nearly 76.5mph. By 1955, the still technically advanced Traction Avant was appearing dated in its styling. Some other aspects of the car were also showing signs of age, such as the three-speed transmission when its contemporaries had four-speed gearboxes. When the DS made its appearance the days of the Traction Avant were clearly numbered, and production ceased immediately in Britain. However, it remained available in France until 1957, by which time nearly 701,000 examples had been built, including a number constructed for French Government and Presidential use.

The Traction Avant was built between 1934 and 1957 and appeared in a variety of engine sizes, chassis lengths and body styles, the saloon depicted here has a long wheelbase and six-cylinder engine. *Malcolm Bobbitt*

Citroën was the Presidential choice of both Coty and de Gaulle, and this fleet of mainly six-cylinder Tractions is pictured outside the Élysée Palace in Paris. For years Citroën was favoured by the French establishment rather than Peugeot, Simca or even the state-owned Renault. For example, President Coty commissioned two State Limousines, one with coachwork by Chapron, the other by Franay. *Citroën*

Two Horses

WHEN the Deux Chevaux, with its promise of minimal motoring costs, was introduced at the Paris Motor Show in October 1948, visitors clamoured to see the fragile-looking car with its corrugated bonnet and fabric covering to roof and boot. Utilitarian beyond belief, the car demonstrated a nose-down attitude, had spindly wheels and prominent headlamps. Inside the car, the canvas clad tubular seats gave no hint of comfort; the absence of instrumentation other than an ammeter and speedometer, the latter strapped to the windscreen pillar, all added to the austerity. A gear lever sprouting from the minimal dashboard accentuated the sober appearance.

Launched in a time of severe raw material shortages, the frugal 2CV with its tiny air-cooled twin-cylinder engine that consumed minimal amounts of petrol was a welcome revelation. A car of its time, it had been conceived in the mid-1930s, shortly after Michelin had acquired Citroën. Pierre Boulanger, in charge of Citroën's day-to-day affairs, having set out to plan future models decided there was a need to produce a simple, yet efficient, economy car that would be both cheap to buy and to maintain.

Work on the project was conducted mainly at Michelin's Clermont-Ferrand factory, rather than at Citroën's Paris works as might have been expected. Pierre Boulanger decreed that the car should accommodate at least two people, a sack of potatoes and a small barrel of wine. Moreover it should be possible to transport a basket of eggs over a ploughed field without any being broken. These criteria proved to be a challenge for Citroën's established engineers who were used to larger and more powerful vehicles. Add to the recipe 90mpg fuel consumption and a top speed in excess of 30mph, and the dilemma facing the design department can be understood.

The appointment of André Lefèbvre to the design team was at Boulanger's insistence, an assurance that the proposed car – known then as the TPV (Toute Petite Voiture) – would be unorthodox. Working under the direction of Marcel Chinon, who was to co-ordinate the TPV project, and Maurice Broglie, head of research at Citroën, Lefèbvre soon decreed that the vehicle should be light in weight with a non load-bearing body; it would have front-wheel drive and soft suspension.

By the end of 1937 a total of 20 prototype cars were ready for testing at Citroën's test track secretly located at La Ferté-Vidame near Dreux in northern France. The vehicles made for a weird sight with their solitary headlamps and simple hammock seats, whilst their corrugated bodies were built from Duralinox

Despite the single headlamp perched on the off-side of the vehicle and the starting handle protruding from the bonnet, the resemblance between the prototype car seen here and the definitive 2CV is obviously apparent. The efforts to develop a 'no-frills' economy car commenced in the mid-1930s, soon after Citroën was acquired by Michelin; the projected launch date being set for 1940. Trials were initially conducted using BMW motorcycle engines, until Citroën engineers devised a water-cooled twin-cylinder unit that was then superseded by one that was air-cooled. *Citroën*

Plans to put the 2CV into production having been interrupted by the hostilities, what emerged post-war was a somewhat different car. The body was more substantial; there were two headlamps and two windscreen wipers, whilst the engine could be started from within the vehicle. The essential qualities as laid down pre-war remained; the 2CV had to be inexpensive to buy and maintain, use minimal fuel and employ the most compliant suspension for comfort even over the roughest surfaces. *Citroën*

The scene at the 1948 Paris Motor Show, with crowds clamouring to see the 2CV, which had arrived at a time of austerity. Last minute changes to engine design meant that cars on show had their bonnets locked. *Citroën*

The 2CV became a way of French life, as seen in this 'still' taken from an episode of BBC Television's *Maigret* detective series of the 1960s, which starred Rupert Davies (standing). This famous sleuth solved many of his cases in Paris to the strains of the accordion, whilst the stirring theme tune to this 60s series was composed by Ron Grainer, who was also responsible for the BBC's *Doctor Who* score. *BBC*

A feature of the 2CV was the canvas roof that could be rolled open to make the most of summer motoring or transport bulky or tall items. Early cars in this range also had fabric boot covers, which were secured beneath the rear window. *Malcolm Bobbitt*

One-piece ripple bonnets were a feature of the 2CVs built before December 1960; those fitted to later models were modified with a revised grille and separate side panels. *Malcolm Bobbitt*

This early 2CV is seen at London's Design Museum as part of an exhibition dedicated to Flaminio Bertoni's automotive styling. A Traction Avant and DS can be seen in the background. *Malcolm Bobbitt*

and magnesium in order to minimise weight while mica replaced glass and waxed canvas replaced roof and doors. Early trials were conducted using 500cc BMW motorcycle engines, though development concentrated on Citroën's own 375cc twin-cylinder water-cooled boxer unit.

By the spring of 1939, the TPV's development was well under way. Boulanger ordered that 250 pre-production examples be constructed in readiness for the model's introduction at the Paris Motor Show planned for later that year; however, due to world events it did not take place. Just as the final batch of vehicles was being finished, the arrival of the German military in France determined Boulanger to instruct that all prototypes be destroyed. When the TPV project was resurrected in 1944-5, it was accepted that the original design was too utilitarian for it to be ever a commercial success. Therefore, Walter Becchia, recruited from Talbot-Lago, was put in charge of engine design, Flaminio Bertoni tended to styling and Marcel Chinon oversaw suspension and road holding.

The design that emerged in 1946 was more akin to the 2CV that most people would recognise today; there were two headlamps, whilst the interior (albeit basic) was comfortable and draught-proof. The coil-sprung suspension, inter-connected front to rear, courtesy of horizontal cylinders located beneath the chassis, offered the softest ride imaginable. At the car's introduction there still remained a question regarding engine design. The vehicles displayed at the Salon all had their bonnets sealed, and for good reason as they were empty! An all-new 375cc horizontally-opposed air-cooled twin cylinder engine was ultimately adopted owing to its compact size and lightness; the absence of a radiator, hoses and water pump added to the ease of maintenance, whilst instant starting, even in freezing conditions, furthered simplicity and reliability.

Intensive testing revealed fuel consumption of 55mpg, a figure reflecting greater vehicle weight than originally specified owing to the use of more substantial materials such as steel and glass rather than alloy and mica. Whereas a pull-cord recoil hand starter operated from the car's interior had been specified, an electro-mechanical device was fitted whereby a lever, connected to a dashboard mounted spring-loaded pull, connected with the starter solenoid. There was preference for a four-speed gearbox, the push-pull gear lever proving to be a lot easier in operation than a conventional selector. Though the car's unpretentious interior easily accommodated four people in comfort, its outward appearance summoned ridicule from the media. Nevertheless, thousands of orders were placed for the car prior to going into production at Citroën's Levallois factory on the western outskirts of Paris.

Shortages of raw materials and lack of industrial resources meant that, by the end of 1949, fewer than 1,000 2CVs had been built. The price of the car escalated, thus mirroring increasing manufacturing costs, yet despite this, hordes of would-be customers flocked to experience the 2CV's 'no-frills' motoring.

With car production earmarked mainly for export, it was not until 1951 that Citroën was able to turn out the 2CV at a rate of around 100 per week, all painted the same grey colour. Domestic deliveries of the 2CV were at first limited to essential users such as priests, doctors and farmers. Production during 1952 rose to some 400 vehicles a week, but the waiting time for a new vehicle never dropped below 18 months. Notwithstanding its 9bhp performance, driving a 2CV was a satisfying experience. The hammock seats offered superlative comfort and the roll-back roof, while providing open-top motoring, also afforded transport for bulky items; thus the 2CV doubled as a load carrier.

The absence of instrumentation in the 2CV was not problematic; the speedometer cable operated the windscreen wipers; a fuel tank dip stick obviated need of a fuel gauge, and upward-hinged front windows facilitated hand signalling as well as ventilating the car's interior. However, minimal engine power made it essential for drivers to maintain maximum revs in order to preserve momentum and a top speed of around 40mph. On straight roads, driving flat out over long distances presented little difficulty, but when it came to negotiating bends it was the suspension that took the strain. Hence it was normal to see 2CVs leaning alarmingly while all four wheels stayed firmly on the ground.

A flat metal boot lid replaced the canvas cover for the 1957/8 model year but some owners opted to fit non-standard boot extension covers as depicted here. *Malcolm Bobbitt*

Below: Despite their fragile appearance 2CVs were rugged vehicles; cars that have been allowed to degenerate to the extent illustrated keep going against all odds. *Malcolm Bobbitt*

Below Right: With their minimal body and interior furnishings, 2CVs still enjoy a loyal following in their native France. The comfort and fuel economy these cars afford is legendary. *Malcolm Bobbitt*

Though a replica, this 2CV captures the essence of the special-bodied car that broke international records in the 350cc class of vehicle at Montlhéry near Paris in 1953. Driven by Vinatier and Barbot, the car averaged 90.960km/h and 85.2km/h over 12- and 24-hours respectively. *Malcolm Bobbitt*

Between the 2CV entering production and the end of the era covered by this book, a number of relatively minor modifications were made to the car's specification. So slight were the changes that to the untrained eye, even late model 2CVs could easily be confused with early examples.

In 1951, the 2CV was given an ignition key and door locks in the interest of security, whilst the following year saw the choice of two shades of grey paint. A year later, the frontal aspect of the 2CV underwent almost inconsequential change when the grille motif lost its oval surround. In 1954, increased power arrived in the form of a 425cc engine; at the same time a centrifugal clutch, automatically disengaging at engine speeds below 1,000rpm, provided for relaxed town driving. Flashing indicators were fitted in the form of single units located on the rear quarter panels. A luxury 2CV featured from 1956, when a heater and demister, better quality upholstery and a larger rear window were specified. In 1957 a metal boot lid rather than the roll-up canvas affair was introduced, and gradually additional colour schemes were offered. For real extravagance, a radio could be specified.

A significant change was made to the 2CV's styling that became effective in December 1960, when the familiar one-piece rippled bonnet with its side cooling louvres made way for a five-rib pressed steel cover featuring a revised grille. Within two years the 2CV's colour range was expanded to include vivid hues to mirror a youthful society and the 'Swinging Sixties'. For 1963 the 2CV's austere image was given another make-over, this time the interior styling now included a facia complete with speedometer and fuel gauge. Electrically operated windscreen wipers replaced the

Top Left: The two-engined 4x4 2CV Sahara has to be one of the most unusual cars. Designed for use by oil companies, this 2CV variant could tackle even the arid Sahara desert. This was achieved by the rear engine driving the back wheels, which could be engaged when negotiating difficult terrain. *Citroën*

Top Right: Like all 2CVs, the Sahara was fitted with simple hammock-type seats, but note the under-seat position of the fuel tank peculiar to this model. *Malcolm Bobbitt*

Right: The Sahara's second engine fitted at the rear of the car; the cooling fan and louvres above the rear wheel arches ventilate the engine. *Citroën publicity*

cable type and no longer worked at a lethargic pace in proportion to the car's speed. French safety regulations that were introduced in 1964 called for the 2CV's front doors to be front-hinged, thus consigning the rear-hinged 'suicide' type to history.

That year, the 2CV became the first production car to wear Michelin's tubeless radial X tyre, the revolutionary tubed X radials having been fitted as standard since the mid-1950s.

Other developments during the early 1960s included the availability of two variants, one being the Mixte having folding rear seats and a rear hatch that was hinged above the window rather than below it. The AZAM was the other to sport previously unseen luxury; included in this version were better quality seat coverings, passenger sun visor incorporating a vanity mirror, external brightwork embellishments and a window built into each of the rear quarter panels.

Production of the 2CV continued until 1990 via a number of derivatives. One of the most interesting models to appear was the twin-engined all-terrain 4x4 Sahara that was developed primarily for use by oil companies. One 425cc engine drove the front wheels for normal road use, the other, mounted aft and engaged when required, drove the rear wheels.

In 1960, the 2CV received a facelift that included a re-styled three-piece bonnet. Another make-over, in 1965, saw introduction of the rear quarter windows. Note the boot extension on the car in the foreground, along with non-standard wheels. *Malcolm Bobbitt*

For many families, the 2CV was an essential means of transport! The acceptability of the Deux Chevaux made it the choice for chic mademoiselles, farmers taking their animals to market, or for superbly comfortable, simple and truly economical day-to-day transport. There was something satisfying about the 2CV's minimal interior furnishings and lack of instrumentation; early examples were denied even a fuel gauge, a fuel tank dipstick adequately serving its purpose. Even the windscreen wipers were connected to the speedometer cable. *Malcolm Bobbitt*

A variant of the 2CV was the Ami 6, often criticised for its looks and voted the world's ugliest car. It was, however, very popular and offered comfortable family motoring when introduced in April 1961. *Malcolm Bobbitt*

Designed to be a luxury version of the 2CV, the Ami 6 sported a 602cc flat-twin engine along with a reverse-rake rear window. *Author's collection*

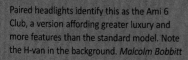

Paired headlights identify this as the Ami 6 Club, a version affording greater luxury and more features than the standard model. Note the H-van in the background. *Malcolm Bobbitt*

Utilising a specially strengthened chassis, the Sahara demonstrated unique climbing abilities owing to its favourable weight distribution. Fewer than 700 examples were built between 1960 and 1966, a number being supplied to Spain's Civil Guardia. Sahara variants were equipped with an auxiliary fuel tank, bonnet-mounted spare wheel, cut-away rear wheel arches and air intakes designed to ventilate the reverse-mounted rear engine.

Aimed at an altogether different market to that of the ubiquitous 2CV was the Ami 6. Designed to fit into the medium class car market, this distinctively styled car has at times been voted the world's ugliest vehicle. Yet, this dubious accolade does not reflect the Ami's comfort, economy and practicality that endeared it to countless families. Introduced in 1961, the Ami with its odd stance and reverse-rake rear window shared the 2CV's technology, albeit with a more powerful 602cc version of its sibling's air-cooled engine. In the autumn of 1964 an estate car variant of the Ami arrived to further the car's already exceptional attributes.

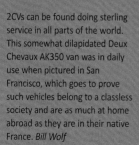

2CVs can be found doing sterling service in all parts of the world. This somewhat dilapidated Deux Chevaux AK350 van was in daily use when pictured in San Francisco, which goes to prove such vehicles belong to a classless society and are as much at home abroad as they are in their native France. *Bill Wolf*

The Goddess

The rush to see the new Citroën, when it was introduced at the Paris Motor Show on 6th October 1955, was unprecedented. It was as if but one exhibit on show, and some 12,000 orders for the DS were taken on the first day, 80,000 by the close of the event! Shown at the Paris Salon was a car with a deftly sculptured aluminium bonnet, the largest such single pressing seen on any motorcar. The traditional air intake having been eliminated, cooling air was sucked into the engine compartment via almost imperceptible scoops beneath the car, the vehicle's smooth underside aiding the streamline effect and improving stability at speed.

Though the motoring world had grown accustomed to unusual offerings from Citroën since the appearance of the Traction Avant and 2CV, the furore in the wake of the DS's arrival was unparalleled, such was the car's futuristic styling.

Under its transcendent clothing, there was unequalled technical specification. This was particularly so with respect to the use of hydropneumatics to perform essential functions such as self-levelling suspension, gear selection, braking and steering assistance. There was nothing new about the concept of pneumatic springing, the idea having excited automotive engineers since the early days of motoring.

What Citroën engineers did was to make this kind of suspension a reliable practicality. The fact that, more than five decades after the DS's introduction, Citroën is still advocating hydraulic suspension for its state-of-the-art luxury saloons says much about the fundamental design.

Apparent in the 1955 car were the deeply curved windscreen and slim front pillars which caused the eye to study the roof line and cantrails, the latter extending rearwards to form cones (known as trompettes) in which the rear indicators were housed. Frameless waist-high doors, the hemlines of which veiled customary sills, furthered the idiosyncratic design, this hemline continuing uninterrupted and concealing the rear wheels, the track of which was narrower than that at the front. The rear indicators successfully camouflaged the

Above Right: The DS 19 was introduced in October 1955 at the Paris Motor Show and was immediately the centre of excitement and controversy. Visitors flocked to see a car that was of radical design and considered to be years ahead of its time. Despite the fact that Citroën did not have cars to deliver, orders flooded in and 12,000 were taken on the first day alone. Development of the DS had been conducted under strict secrecy, and when it was first shown the futuristic styling and use of hydropneumatics were beyond belief. *Citroën*

Features of the DS that helped make it so outstanding were the absence of a traditional radiator grille, the huge aluminium bonnet pressing, frameless windows, glass-fibre roof, partially concealed rear wheels and roof height flashing indicators at the rear. *Citroën*

The construction of the DS was different from any other car and is shown here in 'skeleton' form. Onto the platform is built a frame unit to which the non-load bearing body panels are attached. *Citroën*

The cars seen here are nearing completion at the Quai de Javel factory; note the protective door coverings on this ID19, a less-expensive and lower powered version of the DS, hence the reduced brightwork. *Citroën*

unexpected roof abutment and complemented the deep wrap-around rear screen and boot lid, the latter continuing a downward line to culminate in an unfussy tail. For years, the form of the DS has fascinated vehicle designers and stylists, the majority of whom have been unable to improve on its shape and coefficient drag.

The interior of the DS, with its sculptured dashboard and single-spoke steering wheel, was as extreme as its exterior was radical. The column-mounted gear selector and absence of clutch pedal were indicative of the car's revolutionary engineering, though few spectators were prepared to see a floor-located button masquerading as a brake pedal. Instead of a conventional handbrake, a foot-

The production line at Quai de Javel circa 1956, where DS19s are ready to be driven to the delivery hall ready for despatch to Citroën agents. Notwithstanding the DS's radical engineering, serious technical problems were initially encountered, mainly connected with hydraulics. Once these were addressed and some modifications introduced, the car became noted for its reliability. In this view, Traction Avant cars can be seen on the adjacent assembly line. *Citroën*

operated device with a dashboard-mounted release startled the unsuspecting driver. The car's method of construction and interior layout meant that occupants reclined in spacious comfort, which was more lavish than even the most prestigious limousines could offer.

Work on the DS programme, known officially as 'Project VGD' (Voiture à Grande Diffusion) began pre-war when André Lefèbvre and Flaminio Bertoni looked towards replacing the Traction Avant. Early styling exercises from Bertoni's sketchpad depict an outline of that car with a softer and more streamlined shape overdrawn. At the time motor industry designers were obsessed with streamlining, hence the appearance of delectable cars the like of the Delage D8-120, Delahaye 165, Embericos Bentley, Bugatti 57S and the Lancefield-bodied V12 Lagonda.

Lefèbvre was told by Pierre Boulanger to push design boundaries to the limit in devising the Traction's successor; nothing had to be overlooked or dismissed, however radical or revolutionary the ideas might seem. Surviving sketches show Lefèbvre's preference for a 'tear-drop' shape, which he considered to be aerodynamically perfect.

By the mid 1940s, Bertoni's creation of a sleek wind-cheating shape was to Lefèbvre's satisfaction. Further development materialised in a design known within Citroën as the l'hippopotame (hippopotamus), which was hardly a reference to inspire confidence but was nevertheless submitted to the company's directors at the end of the decade.

When Pierre Boulanger was killed driving an experimental Traction Avant in 1950, Project VGD might well have been jeopardised. Yet, Robert Puiseux, Boulanger's successor, was determined to progress the project and influenced Bertoni to evolve his styling theme to adopt a fastback profile then popular with American manufacturers. Lefèbvre's proposals for the car's construction concentrated around a punt-like platform with front and rear sub-assemblies. Onto this, a skeleton framework (the caisson) supported non load-bearing bolt-on body panels and roof, the latter formed from glass fibre.

Conventionality was further discarded, when Bertoni's interior design called for consigning the traditional dashboard to history and having a handlebar arrangement to substitute for the steering wheel. Unconvinced about the latter, Citroën directors settled for a single-spoke wheel. Suspension and braking technology was undertaken by Paul Magès, whose wartime efforts on load-sensitive braking gave rise to experiments with hydraulic fluid under high pressure, this being the true genesis of Citroën's hydropneumatic system. Magès put his expertise to good effect by trying out hydropneumatics on the 2CV and Traction Avant, a derivative of the latter appearing with self-levelling rear suspension in 1954.

The swept bonnet line, absence of traditional radiator grille, deeply curved front and rear windscreens, smooth underside, slender roof and rear wings that partially concealed the back wheels were features that helped to make the DS unique. More than 50 years after its debut, the car is still aesthetically advanced. *Malcolm Bobbitt*

This publicity picture captures the essence of the DS and exemplifies the car's design, which at the time was radical in the extreme. It was not only the DS's futuristic shape that made it stand apart from other vehicles, its suspension and road-holding were quite beyond anything yet experienced; even snow and ice could not deter from its tenacious qualities. Hydropneumatic suspension ensured the car kept at a constant level, however its load was distributed and whatever the weight, while passengers were cosseted in luxury and comfort exceeding that of the most prestigious marques. *Citroën publicity*

Essentially the system devised for the DS used a high-pressure pump that was belt-driven from the engine camshaft via the water pump pulley to pressurise a gas (nitrogen) accumulator, there being separate accumulators (known as spheres) for each wheel. The fluid, fed from a reservoir in the engine compartment, assisted in providing a pressure of 2,490psi before being returned to its source. Should the pressure fall below 2,090psi, the pump circulated the fluid until normal pressure was achieved. Walter Becchia was assigned to the engine development, his preference being for a compact air-cooled flat-six configuration.

When trials exposed cooling difficulties, Becchia decided to test a water-cooled flat-six, but the low bonnet line demanded the radiator had to be located aft of the engine. When alarming handling characteristics were revealed, and with development time seriously compromised, a last-minute decision was taken to utilise the Traction Avant's

The interior of Citroën's prestigious showroom on the Champs Élysées. The occasion is HM The Queen's visit to Paris in 1957, hence the Union flag and drapes representing the Tricolore. Examples of the DS are nearest the camera, an ID19 on the right.
Citroën

reliable, if somewhat agricultural, 1,911cc engine in modified form. For it to fit beneath the sloping bonnet it was necessary to set the engine so far back that the firewall intruded into the passenger cabin.

Within weeks of the DS being approved for production, and a launch date set to coincide with the 1955 Paris Motor Show, news broke of a German manufacturer's intention to introduce a similarly designed car. Bertoni was ordered to make some last-minute styling changes, which, owing to the advanced stage of tooling, he confined to modifying the roof line and altering the tail.

The DS was likened by the media to a spaceship on introduction and Citroën lost no time building on the theme as depicted in this bizarre publicity item. The DS spaceship in this instance was central to an exhibition staged in Milan in October 1957. *Citroën publicity*

HM The Queen's Rolls-Royce Phantom IV makes a marked contrast to the Citroën DS19s that saw duty at the time of Her Majesty's visit to Paris in 1957. There is some irony in the fact that Citroën influenced technology to the extent that within two decades Rolls-Royce would be employing Citroën self-levelling on its Silver Shadow cars. *Citroën*

The interior of the DS proved to be as idiosyncratic as the car's exterior shape. Bertoni's dashboard design may look futuristic for 1955 standards but compared to what he had originally envisaged it was quite tame. The stylist had initially intended doing away with a conventional steering wheel and using components that would not have looked out of place in an aircraft's cockpit. *Brian Scott-Quinn*

Bertoni's endeavours had resulted in a severe roof abutment, and to camouflage this he produced the charismatic trompettes, which distinctively housed the rear indicators. Another embellishment was the extension of rear reflector housings along the lower wing flanks. Bertoni's drawings are indicative of the speed at which the stylist worked; his sketches depicting the roof and tail modifications are dated January 1955, whilst those showing final embellishments were drawn only weeks from the car's debut.

Nowhere was the DS more adept than on the rally circuit. In most instances, rally drivers specified the ID19, preferring that model's manual gear change and unassisted steering. *Citroën*

38

The DS was developed under such strict secrecy that only a handful of people within Citroën actually knew about the project as a whole. One of those fortunate and trusted personnel was Ken Smith, Chief Engineer at Citroën's British (Slough) factory. It was Ken's job to prepare the works for DS production, his engineering expertise and fluency in French making him the ideal candidate to work in Paris alongside senior members of Citroën's design department. A covert operation was maintained at Citroën's La Ferté-Vidame test track. Concealed from prying journalists, experimental cars gave valuable data regarding the complexities of the hydraulics together with handling and road-holding characteristics. Despite the secrecy, the media obtained news about the forthcoming car and the disclosure added to the excitement of its debut.

From the Grand Palais, a fleet of 20 DS demonstration cars were used to take select clients to the show. Specially trained drivers drove their vehicles to full potential, emphasising the smooth and rapid acceleration with gear changing to match, all with effortless operation of the controls. Drivers kept to a prepared route taking in all road surfaces, including stretches of pavé (cobbles), to verify the

This publicity image evocatively portrays the DS's role as an establishment car so beloved by French government officials. The car is the top-of-the-range DS21 Pallas and its futuristic styling is not out of place amidst the palatial surroundings. The DS was a favourite of General Charles de Gaulle and it was in a car similar to this he survived an attempted assassination as a result of the vehicle's ability to ride on punctured tyres courtesy of its hydraulic suspension system. *Citroën publicity*

In October 2005, in an event organised to celebrate the 50th anniversary of the DS, more than 2,000 examples from throughout the world descended upon Paris. The car illustrated is one of the few surviving British-assembled cars that participated in the occasion.
Malcolm Bobbitt

Photographed near Angers in the mid-1980s, this DS Pallas depicts minor styling changes introduced in September 1962. Modifications amounted to a re-designed air-intake and adoption of rubber over riders. Pallas models were afforded even greater luxury than the otherwise superbly appointed DS.
Malcolm Bobbitt

In addition to the saloon, the DS was built as an estate car, an example of which is pictured in London during the early 1960s. At the time it was introduced, few other shooting brakes had equal or greater carrying capacity. *Citroën*

qualities of the cars' suspension. A British journalist, fortunate to be invited to experience the DS at the time of the Paris Motor Show, recorded what an advanced car the Citroën was, and how it travelled at great speed over rough surfaces with no ill-effect to passengers.

The DS's ability to raise and lower itself, whilst maintaining a constant height when moving, has always evoked fascination. Stronger than steel springs, the hydropneumatic suspension afforded a ride quality impervious to road surface and load carried: it was the proverbial 'magic carpet ride'. Hydraulics facilitated wheel changing, lifting the offending side of the car, even if it meant having to remove a rear wing in the process, itself a simple operation.

Never had a car demonstrated such stopping powers, the use of the floor-located button requiring some practice before perfection of smooth and graduated braking. Oddly, a number of media commentators have criticised the DS's brakes as being too powerful!

As a means of monitoring the car's performance, 500 pre-production units were supplied to selected loyal customers who agreed to become 'pilot users' and provide reliability reports. Problems with hydraulics were quick to manifest, the grave situation determining the manufacturer to despatch squads of engineers – the Super Contrôle – to dispense rapid assistance where and whenever summoned. In time Citroën overcame the problems, but not before a number of technical modifications had to be instigated.

Once the DS was in production its price and complex technology became disincentives to those customers attracted to the car's design but disinclined towards the luxury and intricacies it offered. Addressing the problem, at the 1956 Paris Motor Show Citroën introduced the ID19, a simplified (thus cheaper) model with less reliance on hydraulics.

At first glance the ID19 appeared identical to its sibling though close examination revealed an exterior largely bereft of brightwork and a somewhat frugal interior. Nearly 14% cheaper than its sister-car, price savings were achieved by using less elaborate upholstery materials, sacrificing carpets for rubber matting, specification of a conventional facia and eliminating trim items such as arm rests and roof linings. Notwithstanding these economies, the ID19 was considerably more luxurious and comfortable than most other cars of the day. For customers demanding even more austerity Citroën offered the Normale, which in the interest of economy was even deprived of ashtrays.

Few estate cars had the capacity of the Citroën with its split tailgate lifting clear of the rear hatch. The roof rack was a standard feature and, according to model, the rear section of the vehicle had two side-facing occasional seats. *Citroën publicity*

The ID19 was a de-tuned but more economical version of the DS19, and few seemed to care that its 62bhp engine took longer to accelerate to a top speed of 82.6mph. The manual transmission called for a conventionally operated clutch, the column-mounted selector providing the smoothest gear changing. Braking was largely conventional with a pedal replacing the floor button, and an under-dash handbrake supplanting the foot-operated parking brake. The lack of powered steering summoned major effort when parking, hence the need for a larger diameter steering wheel.

Though the ID outsold the DS, it did little for Citroën's profits owing to its expense of manufacture. In time the specification between the two models narrowed to a point where differences mainly concerned engine and transmission detail. When an estate car derivative of the ID19 was announced in 1958 it was immediately acclaimed for its impressive seating capacity and load carrying ability.

Features included a built-in roof rack and unimpeded interior access, courtesy of the split tailgate, the upper section lifting clear of the rear hatch, the lower dropping to form a loading platform that could be left lowered to support long items. A truly versatile car, some models had retractable side-facing jump seats at the rear while others had three rows of forward-facing seats to accommodate up to as many as eight passengers. Often the choice of larger families and tradesmen, ID19 'breaks' were employed to perform a multitude of uses to include taxicabs, ambulances, hearses, vehicle transporters and camera mounts for film and television purposes.

For many customers, the ultimate DS was the cabriolet constructed by Henri Chapron, whose highly respected coach building business was located at Levallois to the north-west of Paris. Citroën had already anticipated building such a car, but last-minute developments to the saloon and preparing estate models meant the project's indefinite deferment. Citroën initially refused to supply Chapron the necessary DS base units on which to build the cabriolet. Determined to proceed nevertheless, the coach builder purchased complete cars for conversion, the first being shown in 1958. Demand for the cabriolet (Décapotable) was unprecedented, persuading Citroën to review its decision and entrust Chapron with production of a factory-approved (Usine) model to differentiate it from the coach builder's other designs. Despite having a price twice that of the ID19 saloon, the exquisite Décapotable immediately attracted a select clientele and long waiting list.

Specially strengthened DS base units to include running gear and drive-train were delivered to the Levallois works, the ensuing modifications and coach building being hand-crafted. The windscreen surround was reinforced so that it supported the closed hood; new doors were formed, each fabricated from two standard DS units, and an entire rear section comprising wings, boot and hood storage was created.

An aspect of the DS that still attracts so much fascination is the jacking arrangement. To lift one side of a car the suspension has to be fully raised; a stand is placed under the opposite side and the suspension fully dropped to allow the offending wheels to rise. To replace a rear wheel the wing has to be removed – simply by undoing a single bolt. *Citroën*

Depending on model specification, estate cars feature side-facing occasional seats that fold away when not in use. The tailgate lifts clear of the body to allow bulky items to be loaded into the car's capacious interior. *Citroën*

At 2cm longer than the saloons, the cabriolets were luxuriously appointed and finished to individual requirement. A choice of DS or ID specification meant the former having the more powerful engine and semi-automatic transmission, the latter having less power and a conventional gearbox and clutch.

Various modifications were applied to DS and ID cars up to the end of 1964. Among the more essential, grilles known as cendriers (or more informally expressed as 'potato chippers') were fitted to the front wings of DS variants to aid cooling, and in the same year both models received slightly longer rear wings. In 1960 electrical systems were upgraded to 12-volts (12-volt systems were always fitted to UK models), and a year later DS models were given re-styled dashboards. The most significant styling change arrived in 1962. A front-end make-over featured new bumpers with rubber over-riders and also incorporated a modified front apron designed to improve cooling, hence elimination of the wing-top grilles. That year export and cabriolet ID models were equipped with the DS engine, and early in 1963 a manual transmission DS was available while power steering became optional on all ID cars.

Possibly from all the DS models, the most celebrated was the Decapotable. Citroën had intended introducing a 'factory' model, a move that was shelved owing to finding solutions to the DS's many technical problems. French coach builder Henri Chapron, famed for producing fine coachwork on a variety of chassis, seized the opportunity and designed this masterpiece of style. In producing the car, the coach builder had to acquire initially finished vehicles from the manufacturer and undertake the complicated conversion. *Citroën*

Late in 1964, ID19s were given 75bhp engines and redesigned dashboards, but changes were overshadowed by the announcement of a more luxurious DS model, the Pallas. The Pallas exemplified an unsurpassed level of luxury. High-backed seats were sumptuously upholstered, often with the finest hide, while door cappings were leather trimmed and deep pile carpeting extended along the inner sills. Externally the cars were identified by their auxiliary driving lamps, brightwork along door tops and bottoms and around the front indicators, full length rubbing strips, dedicated hubcaps and brushed aluminium rear quarter panels.

Though beyond the era covered in this book, other changes to the DS and ID range included adoption of more powerful engines in 1965, an over-square 1,985cc unit for the DS19 and for the newly announced DS21; a 109bhp 2,175cc affair. In September 1966, non-corrosive green mineral LHM hydraulic fluid universally replaced the red LHS type, but the most important modification occurred in 1967. To coincide with that year's Paris Motor Show, significant re-styling resulted in all DS and IDs featuring new front wings incorporating paired headlights, the innermost (according to model specification) having directional control.

The DS proved itself in motor sport by demonstrating it could survive the rally circuit more ably than some of its competitors; such were the suspension's enduring qualities. It wasn't long before the DS and ID were taking the laurels at the Monte Carlo Rallye and other formidable events, including the East African Safari and the Moroccan and Portuguese rallies.

The DS also heralded development of arguably Citroën's most revered supercar, the Maserati-engined SM which, sadly, was a casualty of the 1970s' oil crisis. Possibly more than anything else, the DS will always be

Below: The DS took on a new image in 1967 when the car's frontal styling was modified to incorporate, according to specification, directional twin headlights that were connected to the vehicle's steering arrangement. The swivelling lights not only gave a wider spread of light, they usefully illuminated the direction of the wheels at corners and road junctions. *Citroën publicity*

Bottom: The DS was in production for 20 years after which time the styling remained as fresh and different as it was excitingly radical when first seen. Not only is the DS visually distinctive today, its ride is superior to that of most modern cars. *Brian Drummond*

associated with the failed assassination attempt on the life of President Charles de Gaulle: when the President's car was attacked and the tyres punctured by weaponry, it was the vehicle's hydropneumatic suspension and stability that enabled it to speed to safety.

The DS has subsequently influenced automotive technology in no small measure. Its suspension was later used by Rolls-Royce and Bentley as a means of self-levelling, and similar suspension technology has been utilised by a number of other vehicle manufacturers. The legacy of the DS ensured the success of later generation Citroën models, and today the car is accepted as a design icon.

'Breaks' were used for a variety of purposes and excelled as ambulances. These vehicles were ideally suited for such work, their commodious interior allowing a stretcher to be easily located within the passenger compartment, and the suspension affording an optimum ride. Citroëns were even used in Britain by the Inter-County Ambulance Service. *Citroën*

As an art form the DS had few rivals, and it evoked Roland Barthes to comment that the car represented the new Nautilus. Whether an art form or advanced automotive design, few cars are as enjoyable to ride in or drive.

Production of the DS continued until the middle of 1975, by which time even more powerful engines had been introduced, the ultimate being a fuel-injected 2.3-litre affair. Differences between ID and DS models were rationalised so that parity existed except mainly for transmission type and engine size. A total of 1,455,746 D-type cars were built, including those that were assembled outside France.

Excitingly different is one of describing the DS's innovative technology, its signature on post-1967 cars being the directional headlights that have become a feature on many current prestige cars. *Citroën publicity*

British-Built Citroën Cars

D URING the 40-years between 1926 and 1966, Citroën also made a significant contribution to Britain's motor industry by assembling in excess of 140,000 cars and Canadian Military Pattern (CMP) lorries at its factory on the Slough Trading Estate in Buckinghamshire. When opened by André Citroën in February 1926, the firm rightly claimed its works to be both the most modern and the largest British car factory space under a single roof, though it should be qualified that the claim was relevant only in respect of floor area and not in terms of production facilities or vehicle output.

The opening of the factory followed the establishment in 1923 of Citroën Cars Ltd., a wholly-owned British subsidiary of the French company, which had a prestigious headquarters at Brook Green near Hammersmith in west London.

The subsidiary had been incorporated to oversee the sale of vehicles, which previously had been undertaken on Citroën's behalf by Gaston Ltd. Assembly at Slough was a means of avoiding Britain's arduous import duties on foreign cars, but required compliance to legislation requiring such vehicles to utilise a large proportion of locally-sourced components. Cars built at Slough, therefore, differed to those made in France by having components and interiors familiar to British motorists.

In addition to the home market, vehicles assembled at Slough were exported to Britain's colonies. Citroën was not the only car maker to have a British assembly facility, as Renault and Fiat also took advantage of these tax concessions. Slough-built Citroën models were highly regarded for their quality and engineering excellence, and were certainly on a par with the like of Riley, Singer, Humber and Rover. When the Traction Avant was introduced, it too was assembled at Slough and the car immediately attracted huge attention, particularly from the motor sport fraternity. Slough-built Tractions were initially assembled using complete body shells brought in from France, the conversion to right-hand drive being undertaken locally.

Traction Avant cars pictured in the early 1950s outside Citroën's factory on the Slough Trading Estate. As well as satisfying the home market, Slough-assembled cars were exported throughout the British Commonwealth. *Citroën*

This Slough-built Light Fifteen was pictured whilst participating in the September 1952 London Rally. The British assembled Light 15s comprised a high percentage of British-sourced components, including radiators, wheels and bumpers. Interiors had wooden dashboards and leather trimmed seats to suit the taste of UK motorists. As this picture implies, the Traction Avant was favoured by the sporting fraternity. *Citroën*

In Britain, the Légère was sold as the Light Fifteen, whilst the Normale, with its longer wheelbase and wider track, was marketed as the Big Fifteen. Like its smaller sibling the Normale (as seen here) featured a hide interior and walnut instrument board. Winter driving presented little difficulty to Citroën vehicles! *Author's collection*

Later, when the necessary jigs were installed, body shells were constructed from panels sent from France and welded together by the oxy-acetylene process, which was followed by lead-loading and painting. Component suppliers to the Slough factory included Bridge of Weir and Connolly (upholstery), Exide (batteries), Fairey Aviation (radiator shells), Lockheed (brakes), Lucas (electrical), Newton & Bennett (dampers), Ripault (wiring) and Smiths (instruments). Meanwhile, Slough had its own carpentry shop to supply the necessary wood trim and facias, along with a dedicated plating shop.

Milestones in the history of Slough's Tractions included the adoption of rack and pinion steering in 1937 and, from the 1938 model year, a particular style of wood facia. For 1939 the Fifteen, introduced in 1935, was marketed as the Big Fifteen, a luxury car in every respect. Announced for 1940 was the Big Fifteen Roadster (five were built, the sole survivor of which was purchased by racing driver Mike Couper). Along with this was a truly magnificent six-cylinder car known as the Six, of which only a few were built. Production of cars stopped during World War II and the factory added to the war effort by assembling Canadian Military Pattern (CMP) lorries and other vehicles from semi-knock-down (SKD) components shipped from Canada. Of the 88,000 CMPs built in Britain, 23,480 were assembled at Slough, the factory operating a three-shift system working 24-hours, seven days a week at times.

Production of cars resumed in early 1946, firstly with the Light Fifteen and then the Six in September 1948. It was not until October 1952 that the Big Fifteen was re-introduced, by which time all Traction Avant models had received the larger boot arrangement. Slough management would have liked to introduce a more modern

Six-cylinder Citroën cars found an enthusiastic clientele who revered their cars for the comfort and performance they afforded. This Slough-built Six would have cost £1,544 12s 3d in 1952, putting it in the Humber Super Snipe and Riley 2.5-litre league. *Malcolm Bobbitt*

Top Left: The Light Fifteen cost £1,067 in 1954 to compete in the UK market with cars such as the Wolseley Four Forty Four, MG Magnette and Peugeot 203, over which it was arguably more technically advanced. *Malcolm Bobbitt*
Top Right: The corporate similarity between the Six H (on the left) and Light Fifteen is clearly evident. The models shared the same fundamental technology, albeit engine size and overall dimensions. *Malcolm Bobbitt*
Right: Slough-assembled 2CVs employed a number of minor differences to their French counterparts, such as chrome bumpers, dedicated bonnet insignia, opening rear windows and a metal boot lid. The example pictured here is Citroën's press car, which was tested by Bill Boddy from the magazine *Motor Sport* in 1953. *David Conway*

looking Traction with faired-in headlamps and side-lights recessed into the front wings, but the French parent company refused to give permission for the re-styling. The ultimate Slough Traction was the Six H which went into production late in 1954, continuing until September 1955. The car 'with its innovative hydraulic rear suspension' was well received by the motoring press, its ride and handling being superior to all other cars. Total post-war production of the Traction Avant accounted for 19,203 vehicles, 16,921 of which were Light Fifteens, 1,254 Sixes and 1,028 Big Fifteens.

Petrol rationing in the wake of World War II and the need for economical motoring should have ensured the 2CV's success when it went into production at Slough in 1953. Despite having a generous proportion of local components, plus styling changes designed to make the car more appealing to British customers, it was far too utilitarian in appearance and appointment. Few motorists appreciated the car's reliability, its frugality, the comfort that the hammock-type seats afforded, and the simplicity of the push-pull gear lever. Being more used to conventional cars, they viewed the little Citroën with suspicion. As a result, no more than 672 2CV saloons were assembled between 1953 and 1960, many of which were exported.

The 2CV was also assembled in van and pick-up versions, the latter unique to Slough. A total of 297 civilian commercial 2CVs were produced, 215 of which were sold on the home market. All the more exceptional was the 2CV pick-up for use with the Royal Marine Commandos, 65 vehicles having been designed to be air-lifted by helicopter from the Royal Navy's commando carriers, HMS *Albion* and HMS *Bulwark*. These pick-ups, built between 1959 and 1961, were constructed specifically for military use and were chosen because of their lightness, ample ground clearance and excellent traction over rough terrain.

Another vehicle unique to the Slough plant was the Bijou, a derivation of the 2CV, which was designed specifically for the British market. There was little to suggest from the car's clothing that it shared any resemblance to the twin-cylinder car, yet underneath the stylish exterior there could be found the, by then, familiar chassis, drive train and running gear. Though designed to compete with some of Britain's other small cars, the Bijou's origins stem from a desire to produce a distinctive small car that took a styling cue from the DS and ID.

The impetus to build the Bijou came from Citroën's Slough Sales Director, Nigel Somerset-Leeke, who foresaw a unique marketing opportunity, which was supported by the parent company in Paris. Advertised as an economical runabout and second car for the more affluent family, the Bijou sported an aerodynamic two-door fibreglass bodyshell, the shape of which was penned by Peter Kirwan Taylor of Lotus fame. For all its chic styling, the Bijou only slightly improved on the 2CV's performance, both in top speed and fuel economy.

For the Slough team, who were obliged to design the car around the 2CV's excellent if minimally-powered engine (Nigel Somerset-Leeke had petitioned Javel for permission to fit a larger engine), the Bijou could be said to be an engineering success. Introduced at the 1959 London Motor Show, production of the Bijou commenced the following summer. Output was optimistically proposed to be 25-30 cars weekly, but in reality a mere 211 cars were built in four years. At a price of £559 compared to the Ford Popular's £509 and the Morris Minor's £553, sadly too few customers were attracted to an attractive if very unconventional car.

The Bijou could not compete with the Mini, which had its debut at the same motor show and cost £47 less. Owing to little knowledge about use of fibreglass for coachwork construction, a number of manufacturing problems were encountered with the Bijou, which led to James Whitsun of West Drayton in Middlesex losing the contract to supply body shells in favour of C. F. Taylor & Co of Crowthorne in Berkshire. With sales lagging behind anticipated demand, production was scaled down and, as soon as all allocated chassis and engines had been used, the Bijou disappeared from the catalogue.

The most difficult enterprise at Slough was introducing the DS. Production of the Traction Avant ceased on announcement of the new car in order that the factory could be reconstructed; this being a huge task overseen by chief engineer Ken Smith.

Ken had already spent much time in France working on the DS project in readiness to assemble the car in England, and it was not until June 1956 that production commenced. It was Ken Smith's task to bring the first right-hand drive DS19 to Britain in time for the 1955 London Motor Show, an exercise that nearly failed.

The plan had been to deliver the car by lorry from Paris via Dunkirk but severe gales in the English Channel meant considerable delays. When shipping resumed after the storms had subsided, commercial vehicles were held back while cars were given priority, had it not been so, the DS could well have missed the opening of the show. Contrary to orders from Paris, Ken arranged to put the car onto the ferry; following disembarkation at Dover he then drove it direct to Slough. In doing this journey he become the first person to drive a DS19 on a public highway, in either France or Britain. During the time taken to install the new production line at Slough, work was undertaken converting Paris-built body shells to right-hand drive and building-up the vehicles with their mechanical apparatus. The exercise proved to be good training for when Slough was fully operational, which was not until early-1957. As with the Traction Avant, production of the Slough DS was maintained with a proportion of UK-sourced components, though not on the same scale as the 2CV.

Right: The 2CV's unique long-travel suspension is wonderfully illustrated in this press photograph, which was taken soon after the car went into production in Britain. The car was too utilitarian for most British motorists. *Author's collection*

Bottom Left: The 2CV appeared as a stylish two-door coupé unique to the Slough factory. Beneath the glass fibre body, styled by Peter Kirwan Taylor of Lotus fame, is the usual 2CV running gear. *Malcolm Bobbitt*

Bottom Right: The Bijou was the brainchild of Nigel Somerset-Leeke, Citroën's Sales' Director. Nigel negotiated unsuccessfully with the parent company in Paris to fit a larger engine to the Bijou rather than the 435cc affair that was employed. *Malcolm Bobbitt*

In order for the DS19 to be assembled at Slough, the British factory had to be re-tooled and UK production of the Traction Avant thus had to be terminated two years ahead of French output. Getting the DS into production at Slough was a mammoth task, which was made all the more difficult owing to the car's advanced technology. The wing top vents aid cooling. *Citroën*

Slough cars differed from their French counterparts by having dedicated seats, radiators, fuel tanks, exhaust systems, instrumentation and electrical components. Externally the cars varied by their rectangular number plate plinths (a legal requirement), the design of the rear indicator housings and tail lamp assemblies, and the Citroën script on the bonnet. Unlike the Paris-built cars, which had fibreglass roofs, those on Slough DS examples were of aluminium.

A pricey car, the DS19 cost more than either a Rover or Jaguar of the same era, and, therefore, there was some reluctance on behalf of motorists to experience the Citroën's innovative engineering. It was for this reason that the less expensive (by £300) but no less luxurious ID19 was introduced in March 1958.

Without power steering and having a manual clutch (with a column-mounted gear lever), a conventional brake pedal and braking system, together with a handcrafted wood dashboard, hide upholstery and two-tone paint scheme, the ID19 appealed to a far wider market. The Safari estate car was also well received when introduced in 1960, for no other vehicle of its type offered such generous accommodation or carrying capacity. An eight-seater Tourmaster was added to the catalogue in 1964, and additionally a Countryman version finished by coach builder Harold Radford was offered. The Safari was also marketed as an ambulance or hearse.

Above: The DS's advanced shape and complicated engineering meant that sales were mainly the preserve of only the most adventurous of British motorists. *Guy Pursey*

Top Right: Slough-assembled estate cars were marketed as the Safari and (like French cars) they featured a built-in roof rack; the upright number plate plinth complies with UK legislation. *Citroën*

Right: Slough-built cars featured the Citroën script on the left hand side of the bonnet and the roofs were aluminium rather than glassfibre. *Citroën*

Slough also built versions of the DS that had no French equivalent, the DS19M and DW, both of which used the DS's mechanical and hydraulic systems coupled with manual transmission. For the sporting customer a high-performance ID19, in the guise of the Connaught GT was offered by Connaught Cars Ltd. of Send in Surrey. An independent conversion, the package included sports-type bucket seats, a high-compression engine, lightened flywheel, twin SU or Solex carburettors and an electric cooling fan. When the DS Pallas was introduced in France in September 1964, there was not a Slough equivalent. When, however, the DS21 came along in September 1965, Slough produced a Pallas version of that car.

By then the French parent company had determined the cost of having a British factory was untenable, and the decision was taken to close it. The last car rolled off the assembly line on 18th February 1966, so ending 40-years production. During the post-war years some 30,000 vehicles were assembled at Slough but after the factory closure all British market cars were supplied direct from France. The Slough works remained as a distribution centre and parts stockist for some time, before being sold to Mars Limited who of course are best known for their brands of confectionery.

Commercial Vehicles

U NTIL 1930, Citroën built commercial models on chassis, albeit suitably modified, that had already been utilised for the firm's car range. For the 1931 model year, the car maker entered the heavyweight market with an 1,800 and a 2,000kg chassis, and a year later the formation of La Société Anonyme des Transports Citroën provided for a dependable network of coach services throughout France. When, in 1937, Citroën became the first motor manufacturer to offer a diesel-engined vehicle, demand for the company's commercial products multiplled.

In Britain, during the 1920s and '30s, Citroën taxis were a familiar sight in London. Highly regarded for their performance and reliability, the Citroën taxi cabs competed with the likes of the conventional Austin and Beardmore models and were employed by some of the leading operators as well as being favoured by many owner-drivers.

When Citroën promoted its commercial vehicles to bus and coach and haulage operators during the early-1930s, Citroën Cars Ltd. exhibited its products at commercial vehicle motor shows. If Citroën had hoped that its commercial operation would enjoy similar levels of success to that of its motorcars, there was to be disappointment. Though the product range was modelled for customer need, clients were more in favour of buying the like of Bedford, Chevrolet and Morris Commercial.

Post-war, the second half of the 1940s saw French production resumed with the pre-war Type 23 in 1,500kg, 1,800kg and two-tonne formats; the series of vehicles being powered by the reliable but somewhat agricultural 1,911cc engine as fitted to the Traction Avant. Also to reappear was the similarly styled but larger six-cylinder 4,580cc Type 45 that had been introduced in October 1934. Both chassis types proliferated as pick-ups, delivery wagons, tipper lorries, petrol tankers, fire tenders, tow trucks and public service vehicles. These vehicles, along with those made by Renault, Berliet and Peugeot, were a familiar sight throughout Europe.

The 2CV Camionnette made its debut in 1952, when this view was taken. In this instance it is serving as a bill sticker's mode of transport, but commercial 2CV variants like this were popular with tradesmen and farmers. Owners all appreciated the vehicle's frugal fuel economy courtesy of its 375cc air-cooled engine and ease of maintenance. *Author's collection*

Commercial vehicles were included in Citroën's catalogue from 1919 but utility variants of the Traction Avant were few owing to availability of the H and 2CV vans, not to mention the range of heavier commercials. The vehicle illustrated is the product of Citroën's Danish organisation and carries the original type of wooden-slatted rear door. Similar vehicles to this had a side-hinged door owing to the roll-type affair proving troublesome. *Brian Scott-Qiunn*

This publicity illustration clearly advocates the 2CV van's fuel economy. Despite the benefits of front-wheel drive and such frugality, which extended to the vehicle's interior appointment, few of these Slough-assembled commercials were sold, customers instead preferring the conventionality of Ford, Austin and Morris amongst other British-built vans. *Citroën publicity*

With the introduction of a new range of commercials for 1955, model designations changed to U23 for the four-cylinder models and Type 55 for the six-cylinder models; the latter also obtainable as a tractor unit. Sharing comparable design cabs with full-width frontal styling and alligator bonnets emblazoned with the double chevron, both chasses were available to specialist coachbuilders. Type 55 vehicles could be specified in 4x4 format for all-terrain work, but all the more revolutionary was the Type 60 with its hydropneumatic suspension. Vehicles were also built for military use, one such being the FOM (Forces d'Outre-Mer), which was available as a three- or five-tonner and fitted with either a 5.1-litre petrol or diesel engine.

Highly regarded for their all-terrain ability, FOMs were specified for use in French Equatorial Africa but eventually modified versions were marketed for civil operations. A number of military FOMs were supplied with auxiliary 500-litre fuel tanks, an essential aid for exploration work in remote areas.

Left: Pictured outside the Hotel de la Plage at Wissant near Boulogne, this Citroën bus is typical of the many that saw service throughout France during the early post-war years. Apparent is the corporate styling of the time that shared a similarity with the Traction Avant. *Malcolm Bobbitt*

Bottom Left The same vehicle as pictured above, which was built on the Type 23 chassis that had been introduced during the 1930s. The Type 23 was built in a variety of body configurations to include pick-ups and delivery wagons, but all were powered by a choice of 1,911cc four-cylinder petrol or diesel engines. *Malcolm Bobbitt*

Bottom Right: The H-van with its corrugated looks was, for a long period, Citroën's workhorse and years after the model ceased production countless examples continue to provide faultless service. This early vehicle, typified by its split windscreen, was recently photographed at the famous Beaulieu Autojumble. *Malcolm Bobbitt*

Notwithstanding the success of the heavyweights, it is the lightweight models that were all the more familiar. As few commercial variants of the Traction Avant were built, the 2CV and H-van represented the mainstay of Citroën's more modest post-war utility vehicles, these becoming an established sight throughout Europe. An alternative to the horse and cart, the corrugated appearance of the 250kg payload 2CV Fourgonnette immediately summoned disparaging comments, with some likening it to a Nissen hut or chicken coop. Such ribaldry became intrinsic to the vehicle's character, and, despite this, large numbers were employed by many European institutions to include the French and Belgian Post Offices and the Netherlands' equivalent of the Automobile Association.

The 2CV chassis, having already proved itself in the domestic sector, was strengthened for load-carrying purposes and its ground clearance increased; the fuel tank was moved to the right hand side of the body aft of the cab, the spare

Right: Owing to its shape (a box on wheels) the H-van attracted the name Cube Utile. The corrugated panels were so formed to give the vehicle, with its unitary construction, its necessary strength. Modern features included front-wheel drive, a side sliding load compartment door and a top-hinged rear hatch. *Malcolm Bobbitt*

Bottom Left: H-vans were used extensively by the emergency services as police vehicles, ambulances and as depicted here, fire tenders. The low floor afforded easy access to the vehicle interior while front-wheel drive assured excellent road holding. Note the suicide cab doors, 2CV headlights pinned to the stubby nose, and a 2CV Camionnette in the background. *Malcolm Bobbitt*

Bottom Right: H-vans were built between 1948 and 1981, and would eventually total more than 473,000 examples. Both petrol and diesel engines featured and in addition to factory models, chassis were made available to specialist coach builders. This BBC photograph shows an H-van during the making of a *Maigret* episode. *BBC*

Superseding the Type 23 in the early 1950s, the U23 featured modern styling. Like its predecessor a range of body configurations were offered to include pick-up, tipper and delivery wagon in addition to special purpose types such as buses. Powered by Citroën's 1,911cc engine, the U23 was available in a choice of three payloads, from 3,500 to 5,000kg. *Author's collection*

wheel oppositely located behind a lift-up hatch. With its flat floor designed to afford maximum load space, the vehicle's merits, especially its economy and reliability were quickly appreciated by its owners and drivers.

The simplicity of the air-cooled flat-twin engine was perfect for commercial work as it could run tirelessly around the clock, whatever the season, whilst requiring only minimal attention. The 2CV van really was intrinsic to French economy; no self-respecting boulanger, pâtissier or vigneron was without a well-worn example.

Relatively few modifications were applied to the 2CV van during its production life. The more powerful 425cc engine was specified from 1954, after which the original AU became the AZU; the new style bonnet seen on the saloon was fitted from July 1961, whilst from March 1963 the body lost its corrugations above the waistline but gained side windows, which previously had been optional. At the same time rearward visibility was improved by elimination of the narrow lozenge-shaped rear door windows in favour of larger rectangular types.

A larger-engined version of the AZU, the AK350 with its 350kg payload, was offered in April 1964 and sold alongside the existing model. Identified by a longer body overhanging the rear wheels, the vehicle was powered by the 602cc Ami 6 engine, in order to give improved performance and the ability to cope with the augmented payload. Universally acclaimed was the AK400, a derivative of the AK350 but with increased carrying capacity courtesy of its high roof configuration. From the spring of 1978 the 2CV Fourgonnette was replaced by the Dyane 6-based Acadiane with its 480kg payload.

A derivative of the AZU was the 'combi' Weekend model that featured large side windows and removable rear seats. Needless to say this 2CV derivative was popular with traders, especially those who wanted a commercial vehicle during the week that they then could easily transform into a family car at weekends. It was also well-liked by motorists who wanted the versatility of a family car with an

Citroën's range of heavy and special purpose commercials included a powerful all-terrain 4x4 vehicle designated Type 55, which was introduced in the mid 1950s. Such models served a variety of purposes, as tipper lorries as depicted here, or as rescue vehicles in service with fire brigades and civil defence units. They were also used for snow clearing. Powered by 4.6 litre diesel engines, Type 55 Sahara versions, with their all-wheel drive, were capable of crossing the roughest ground and for this reason were often specified for oil and gas exploration work. *Citroën (both)*

ability to accommodate lots of luggage, thus the Weekend became the tool for 2CV campervan conversions. Not least, 'Weekend models' were also a popular choice for the hippie fraternity, especially those whose lifestyle led them to embark upon long overland treks with minimal fuss and expense; as a result this variant quickly became synonymous with 'flower power' in the 1960s.

Few vehicles were as distinctive as Citroën's ubiquitous H-van, which made its debut in June 1947. However, its origins went back to 1939 when a forward-control van, known as Le T.U.B., was introduced before its production was curtailed at the onset of war. Designed as a simple cube on wheels (hence the Type H being known as the Cube Utile), this wonderfully practical corrugated box on wheels became an essential part of everyday French life. Like its smaller sibling it was the choice of farmers, food purveyors, commodity manufacturers, traders, builders, fire brigades, ambulance services and even the police. There was not a market place in France, Belgium or Holland where the H-van was conspicuous by its absence. On market day armies of H-vans would arrive to deliver everything from fish, meats and vegetables to clothes and household wares. They also performed an essential role as the omnipresent friterie.

The need to derive the greatest strength from limited supplies of the thin-gauge metal that were available in the early post-war years resulted in the H-van's characteristic appearance. Moreover, building the vehicle in quantity meant employing simple assembly techniques without need of complicated or costly tooling in an effort to economise on steel. The vehicle's punt-like platform gained

Above: Type 55s were available with five-tonne payloads and were fitted with a choice of six-cylinder 4.58-litre petrol or 5.18-litre Diesel Type 100 engines that were introduced in 1959. Eight body styles were offered, some (to include that shown left) with a choice of three wheelbase lengths, 3.6m, 4.6m or 5.33m, in addition to a tractor unit; each having a five-speed gearbox. This wonderfully evocative publicity photograph ably illustrates the 'tracteur routier' with trailer attached transporting a large and heavy piece of machinery. It also shows the ease, and apparent nonchalance, with which the driver is manoeuvring his charge. There is no indication as to where the photograph was taken but it is a strong possibility that the tracteur with its Paris registration is a Citroën demonstrator on exercise at Quai de Javel. Such tractor units fulfiled many roles, including oil tanker haulage. *Citroën*

its strength courtesy of criss-cross members, whilst for added stiffness side longerons formed hollow sections that were used to accommodate the fuel tank on the right hand side, and the spare wheel on the left.

Not least of the H-van's many virtues was its capacious interior with a low floor that facilitated loading that allowed a person to stand upright. The spacious walk-through cab with forward-control was another major benefit made possible by the unitary construction, torsion bar suspension and front-wheel drive, the latter with rack and pinion steering borrowed from the Traction Avant. A sliding side door aided kerbside loading and unloading, and the rear top-hinged hatch and double side-hinged doors were additional features that made this unique mobile cube such an attractive business proposition.

The H-van's utilitarian appearance was intensified by having 2CV style headlights attached to the nose of the stubby bonnet, itself decorated with the double chevron. The bonnet's lift-up front panel gave access to the radiator, but engine maintenance was effected from within the cab by removing the engine cover. Due to its forward-control, the engine was fitted forwards with the gearbox aft, and should the need arise for maintenance purposes the entire drive train could be simply pulled forward by raising the front of the vehicle.

Small (17") wheels, positioned at the extremities of the chassis, helped give the H-van a low centre of gravity, while front-wheel drive and torsion bar suspension afforded exceptional stability and handling characteristics. Engine torque and three-speed transmission made for excellent urban performance, though the steering, which was light enough under most conditions, called for much effort when manoeuvring at low speeds.

The top speed of a little over 50mph was hardly inspiring, and then there was the intrusive engine cacophony, but this amounted to a small price to pay for an outstandingly willing workhorse. In addition to it being supplied in a number of body configurations, the H-type chassis was supplied to coachbuilders to meet specialist and individual requirements. Thus, during the vehicle's 33-year production span, countless styles of coachwork were seen, including mini-buses, camper vans, promotional vehicles, and not least mobile market stalls.

Few technical modifications were made to the H-van during its lifetime. Within two years of its introduction, the 1,200kg payload vehicle was joined by one of 850kg, and another of 1,500kg, the original version being withdrawn in the autumn of 1958, when the 1,500kg model was designed to accept a 2,925kg payload.

The face of the H-van changed in February 1964, when the split windscreen gave way to a single-piece affair, followed (only months later) by the dominant chevrons being reduced in size. A total of nearly half-a-million H-vans were built, their versatility, not least idiosyncratic styling, legendary reliability and characteristic handling, having in recent years made them attractive as camping-car conversions and publicity vehicles.

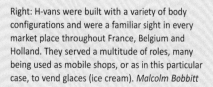

Right: H-vans were built with a variety of body configurations and were a familiar sight in every market place throughout France, Belgium and Holland. They served a multitude of roles, many being used as mobile shops, or as in this particular case, to vend glaces (ice cream). *Malcolm Bobbitt*

Index